What is...
Physician
Contracting
in Healthcare
Organizations?

PAMELA H. DEL NEGRO

AMERICAN BAR ASSOCIATION
Health Law Section

Cover design by Monica Alejo/ABA Design.

The materials contained herein represent the opinions of the authors and editors and should not be construed to be the views or opinions of the law firms or companies with whom such persons are in partnership with, associated with, or employed by, nor of the American Bar Association or the Section of Health Law unless adopted pursuant to the bylaws of the Association.

Nothing contained in this book is to be considered as the rendering of legal advice for specific cases, and readers are responsible for obtaining such advice from their own legal counsel. This book and any forms and agreements herein are intended for educational and informational purposes only.

Printed in the United States of America.

19 18 17 16 15   5 4 3 2 1

ISBN: 978-1-62722-966-1

e-ISBN: 978-1-62722-967-8

Library of Congress Cataloging-in-Publication Data

Del Negro, Pamela H., author.
  What is physician contracting in healthcare organizations? / by Pamela H. del Negro.
      pages cm
  Includes bibliographical references.
  ISBN 978-1-62722-966-1 (alk. paper)
  1. Physicians–Employment–United States. 2. Health facilities–Employees-
-Legal status, laws, etc.–United States. 3. Physicians–Recruiting–Law and legislation–United States. 4. Group medical practice–Law and legislation-
-United States. 5. Medical care–Finance–Law and legislation–United States.
6. Labor contract–United States. 7. Medical laws and legislation–United States. I. Title.
  KF2905.N44 2015
  344.7303'21–dc23

                               2015013065

Discounts are available for books ordered in bulk. Special consideration is given to state bars, CLE programs, and other bar-related organizations. Inquire at Book Publishing, ABA Publishing, American Bar Association, 321 N. Clark Street, Chicago, Illinois 60654-7598.

www.ShopABA.org

Contents

Introduction

Healthcare providers and healthcare facilities operate in a complex and evolving legal and regulatory environment. When the parties to an agreement include one or more physicians and healthcare organizations, contractual arrangements that in other environments involve little or no regulation are often subject to a variety of federal and state laws, rules, and regulations. This book provides an overview of common legal and regulatory issues involved in employment contracts and service agreements between physicians and healthcare organizations for clinical and administrative services.

Given the many types of healthcare organizations and physician specialties and subspecialties that exist in healthcare today, it is no surprise that arrangements between physicians and healthcare organizations can take several forms. Single- and multispecialty physician groups, hospitals and their physician practice group affiliates, long-term-care facilities, ambulatory care centers, urgent-care clinics, federally qualified health centers, and other healthcare organizations rely on physicians to deliver patient care or perform other clinical or administrative duties. In some instances, physicians provide services as an employee of the healthcare organization. In other instances, physicians provide services as an independent contractor to a healthcare organization. These services may be provided through a direct arrangement between the healthcare organization and the physician or through an arrangement between the healthcare organization and the physician's employer. The structure of the arrangement depends in part on the business objectives of the parties and the legal and regulatory framework within which they operate. A hospital that requires the services of physicians to provide call-coverage services for a particular specialty may find it more convenient to contract with a physician group of sufficient size to meet all of the hospital's coverage needs, rather than with several individual physicians. A nursing home or mental health center may prefer to contract directly with the physician that it believes is best suited to serve the unique needs of its patient population rather than with the physician's employer. While employment and clinical and administrative services agreements are the focus of this book, there are many other types of arrangements, each with its own legal and regulatory considerations. These include arrangements with managed-care organizations, co-management agreements, arrangements with accountable care organizations, office space or equipment leases between physicians and healthcare organizations, and medical practice acquisitions. While some of the general principles described in this book may apply to one or more of these arrangements, each arrangement is subject to its own legal and regulatory requirements that are beyond the scope of these pages.

This book describes some of the key legal and regulatory issues that lawyers should consider when drafting employment and clinical and administrative services agreements between physicians and healthcare organizations. Chapter 1 provides an overview of regulatory issues in physician contracting, including the Stark Law, the Anti-kickback Statute, civil monetary penalties, and issues related to contracting with tax-exempt organizations. Chapter 2 discusses contractual considerations for both employment and service agreements and contains sample language for certain contractual provisions. Chapter 3 is a checklist that is intended to serve as a quick reference guide for lawyers drafting and reviewing physician contracts. Chapter 4 contains sample term-sheet provisions for a physician employment agreement. Many of the issues discussed in this book, such as the Stark Law and the Anti-kickback Statute, are sufficiently detailed or complex to warrant their own books. Readers are encouraged to further explore the commentary and resources provided in the footnotes, and to conduct their own independent research, to gain additional insight and understanding into this complex and evolving area of law.

Regulatory Issues in Physician Contracting

1

This chapter provides an overview of key statutes and regulations that lawyers should consider when structuring arrangements between physicians and healthcare organizations. This chapter begins with a discussion of the Stark Law, the Anti-kickback Statute, and civil monetary penalties, each of which imposes substantial restrictions on the type and structure of physician–healthcare organization arrangements. This chapter continues with a discussion of additional considerations when contracting with a tax-exempt hospital or other healthcare organization. Finally, because many states regulate a variety of physician conduct, this chapter concludes with a brief overview of key areas of state-law regulation and enforcement.

The Stark Law

Overview
The federal Ethics in Patient Referrals Law, commonly referred to as the Stark Law, prohibits a physician from referring to an entity for designated health services (DHS)

payable by Medicare or Medicaid with which the physician or his or her immediate family member has a financial relationship, unless an exception applies.[1] If there is a referral as described above, and no exception applies, then the entity that provided the DHS is prohibited from billing for those services.

A referral exists if a physician orders DHS that will not be personally performed by him or her.[2] DHS include:

- clinical laboratory services
- physical therapy services
- occupational therapy services
- radiology services, including magnetic resonance imaging, computerized axial tomography scans, and ultrasound services
- radiation therapy services and supplies
- durable medical equipment and supplies
- parenteral and enteral nutrients, equipment, and supplies
- prosthetic, orthotic, and prosthetic devices and supplies
- home health services
- outpatient prescription drugs
- inpatient and outpatient hospital services
- outpatient speech-language pathology services[3]

If there are referrals for DHS paid for by Medicare or Medicaid, then the next step is to determine whether there is a financial relationship between the referring physician or an immediate family member and the entity to which the physician refers. For purposes of the Stark Law, an "entity" includes the person or organization that performs the service and, if different, the person or organization that bills Medicare for the service.[4] A financial relationship includes an ownership or investment interest in, or a compensation arrangement with, the entity accepting the referral, whether direct or indirect.[5]

In pertinent part, a direct ownership or investment interest exists if the referring physician or an immediate family member has an ownership or investment interest in the entity furnishing DHS without any intervening persons or entities between the two

parties. An ownership or investment interest includes the ownership of stock in a DHS entity, as well as holding a limited liability
company membership in a DHS entity. An indirect ownership or
investment relationship exists if two conditions are met: first,
"[b]etween the referring physician (or immediate family member)
and the entity furnishing DHS there exists an unbroken chain of
any number (but no fewer than one) of persons or entities having ownership or investment interests" that create an indirect
ownership or investment interest by the physician in the entity
furnishing DHS;[6] second, "[t]he entity furnishing DHS has actual
knowledge of, or acts in reckless disregard or deliberate igno-
rance of, the fact that the referring physician (or immediate family
member) has some ownership or investment interest (through
any number of intermediary ownership or investment interests)
in the entity furnishing the DHS."[7] Ownership in a subsidiary is
not considered ownership in the parent company, or in any other
subsidiary, unless the subsidiary has an ownership or investment
interest in the parent or such other subsidiary.[8]

A compensation arrangement exists when there is remuneration
between a physician and an entity.[9] For purposes of the Stark Law,
the term "remuneration" generally includes any monetary payment or nonmonetary benefit made directly or indirectly between
parties.[10] A physician has a direct compensation arrangement with
an entity "if remuneration passes between the referring physician (or a member of his or her immediate family) and the entity
furnishing DHS without any intervening persons or entities."[11]
With respect to a physician who owns an interest in a physician
practice, if such ownership or investment interest includes the
right to receive the financial benefits of the ownership or investment, then the physician is deemed to "stand in the shoes" of
the practice for purposes of this analysis.[12] This means that the
physician has the same compensation arrangements as the physician practice.[13]

An indirect compensation arrangement exists if three requirements are met.

First:

> [b]etween the referring physician (or a member of his or her immediate family) and the entity furnishing DHS there exists an unbroken chain of any number (but not fewer than one) of persons or entities that have financial relationships . . . between them (that is, each link in the chain has either an ownership or investment interest or a compensation arrangement with the preceding link).[14]

"The links in the chain [can] be any form of financial relationship, whether excepted or not."[15]

Second:

> [t]he referring physician (or immediate family member) receives aggregate compensation from the person or entity in the chain with which the physician (or immediate family member) has a direct financial relationship that varies with, or otherwise takes into account, the volume or value of referrals or other business generated by the referring physician for the entity furnishing the DHS.[16]

Third:

> [t]he entity furnishing DHS has actual knowledge of, or acts in reckless disregard or deliberate ignorance of, the fact that the referring physician (or immediate family member) receives aggregate compensation that varies with, or takes into account, the volume or value of referrals or other business generated by the referring physician for the entity furnishing the DHS.[17]

Depending on the relationships that exist between a physician and a healthcare organization, performing a Stark analysis can be a difficult and laborious task. If the analysis determines that there is a financial relationship between the parties, the next step is to determine whether an exception applies. There are exceptions for ownership and investment interests, as well as exceptions for compensation interests. The following discussion is limited to those exceptions most commonly used for employment or service agreements.[18]

Exceptions

An arrangement must meet all of the requirements of an exception in order for the physician's referrals for DHS to be permitted to bill for such services.

Bona Fide Employment Relationships Exception

To satisfy the bona fide employment relationships exception, an arrangement must meet all of the following requirements:

- The employment must be for identifiable services.
- Compensation must be consistent with fair market value and not determined in a manner that directly or indirectly takes into account the volume or value of the physician's referrals.
- The agreement would be commercially reasonable even if there were no referrals.[19]

While the bona fide employment relationships exception does not require the arrangement to be in writing, documenting the arrangement can provide both parties with clarity regarding their respective rights and obligations.

Personal Service Arrangements Exception

Parties entering into arrangements in which a physician or medical practice provides medical director, consulting, or other administrative or clinical services to a hospital or other healthcare entity often look to meet the personal service arrangements exception for purposes of Stark Law compliance. To satisfy the personal service arrangements exception, the arrangement must meet all of the following requirements:

- The arrangement must be in writing, be signed by the parties, and describe the services covered by the arrangement.
- All of the services to be provided by the physician or an immediate family member must be included in the agreement, or, if there is more than one arrangement between the parties, the agreements must incorporate each other by reference or cross-reference a master list of contracts.
- The aggregate services contracted for does not exceed those that are reasonable and necessary for the legitimate business purposes of the arrangement.
- The term of the arrangement is for at least one year.
- The compensation is set in advance, does not exceed fair market value, and (except in the case of a physician incentive plan) is not determined in a manner that takes into account the volume or value of any referrals or other business generated between the parties.
- The services do not involve the counseling or promotion of a business arrangement that violates any federal or state law.[20]

To satisfy the requirement for a one-year term, if the arrangement is terminated prior to the expiration of the first year, the parties may not enter into the same or substantially the same arrangement until the expiration of the one-year period.[21]

Fair Market Value Compensation Exception

The fair market value compensation exception may also be available for arrangements between physicians and healthcare organizations. To satisfy this exception, all of the following requirements must be met:

- The arrangement must be in writing, be signed by the parties, and cover only identifiable items or services.
- The arrangement must include a term. The term can be for any period of time and contain a termination clause, as long as the parties enter into only one arrangement for the same items or services during the course of a year.[22]

- Compensation must be set in advance, included in the agreement, and be consistent with fair market value and not determined in a manner that takes into account the volume or value of referrals or other business generated by the physician.
- The arrangement must be commercially reasonable and in furtherance of the parties' legitimate business purposes.
- The arrangement must not violate the Anti-kickback Statute or federal or state laws regarding billing or claims submission.
- The services must not involve the counseling or promotion of a business arrangement or other activity that violates federal or state law.[23]

The Stark Law is a strict-liability statute. If an arrangement involves physician referrals for DHS, payable by Medicare or Medicaid to an entity with which the physician or an immediate family member has a financial relationship, and no exception applies, then the government can impose civil monetary penalties and even exclude parties from participating in federal healthcare programs.

Anti-kickback Statute

The Anti-kickback Statute prohibits the knowing and willful offering, paying, soliciting, or receiving of remuneration in order to induce a party to (1) refer an individual for goods or services payable by a federal healthcare program or (2) purchase, lease, order, arrange for or recommend the purchase, lease, or order of goods or services payable by a federal healthcare program.[24] The term "remuneration" is generally interpreted to mean "the transfer of anything of value, directly or indirectly, overtly or covertly, in cash or in kind."[25] Both sides of an impermissible "kickback" transaction can be held liable for violations. Violations of the Anti-kickback Statute can subject the parties to both civil and criminal penalties, including exclusion from participation in federal healthcare programs. The Office of Inspector General (OIG) of the U.S. Department of Health and Human Services

(HHS) has, under statutory authority, promulgated safe harbors that can protect an arrangement from prosecution under the Anti-kickback Statute. The arrangement must satisfy all elements of the applicable safe harbor in order to be eligible for such protection. Unlike the Stark Law, failure to meet all elements of an Anti-kickback Statute safe harbor does not necessarily mean that the arrangement is prohibited. However, arrangements that do not satisfy a safe harbor can be subjected to increased scrutiny for compliance with the Anti-kickback Statute.

The Anti-kickback Statute contains a safe harbor for employees.[26] Under the employee safe harbor,

> remuneration does not include any amount paid by an employer to an employee, who has a bona fide employment relationship with the employer, for employment in the furnishing of any item or service for which payment may be made in whole or in part under Medicare, Medicaid, or other Federal healthcare programs.[27]

The employee safe harbor adopts the definition of "employee" from the Internal Revenue Code.[28]

The Anti-kickback Statute also contains a safe harbor for personal services and management contracts. Under this safe harbor, remuneration does not include any payment made by a principal to an agent as compensation for the services of the agent, as long as all of the following standards are met:

- The agency agreement is set out in writing and signed by the parties.
- The agency agreement covers all of the services the agent provides to the principal for the term of the agreement and specifies the services to be provided by the agent.
- If the agency agreement is intended to provide for the services of the agent on a periodic, sporadic, or part-time basis, rather than on a full-time basis for the term of the agreement, the agreement

specifies exactly the schedule of such intervals, their precise length, and the exact charge for such intervals.

- The term of the agreement is for not less than one year.
- The aggregate compensation paid to the agent over the term of the agreement is set in advance, is consistent with fair market value in arm's-length transactions, and is not determined in a manner that takes into account the volume or value of any referrals or other business generated between the parties for which payment may be made in whole or in part under Medicare, Medicaid, or other federal healthcare programs.
- The services performed under the agreement do not involve the counseling or promotion of a business arrangement or other activity that violates any state or federal law.
- The aggregate services contracted for do not exceed those that are reasonably necessary to accomplish the commercially reasonable business purpose of the services.[29]

Under the safe harbor, the term "agent" means a person who has an agreement to provide services for (or on behalf of) the principal, other than in the capacity as an employee.[30] The OIG has issued special fraud alerts, advisory opinions, and other publications that, while not binding, provide guidance on the types of arrangements that will receive scrutiny under the Anti-kickback Statute.[31]

Civil Monetary Penalties

HHS has authority to seek civil monetary penalties (CMPs) for a wide variety of conduct. Notably in this context, CMPs may be assessed against persons and organizations that knowingly make payments to physicians to reduce or limit items or services provided to Medicare or Medicaid beneficiaries under the physician's direct care.[32]

Anti-markup Rule

The federal anti-markup rule limits the ability of physicians to purchase certain diagnostic tests performed by other physicians with whom they do not share a practice and to bill for the professional component (PC) or technical component (TC) of those tests at a higher rate than the physician paid for such tests.[33] A physician is deemed to be sharing a practice with the billing physician (or other supplier) if the physician "is an owner, employee or independent contractor of the billing physician or other supplier and the TC or PC is performed in the office of the billing physician or other supplier."[34] If the anti-markup rule applies, then the billing physician must be paid the lesser of the performing physician's (or supplier's) actual charge, the billing physician's (or supplier's) actual charge, or the applicable fee schedule amount.[35]

Contracting with Tax-Exempt Organizations

Contractual arrangements between physicians and tax-exempt healthcare organizations can impose additional requirements on the parties. IRS regulations generally prohibit any portion of a tax-exempt hospital's earnings from inuring to the benefit of a private party. Compensation must be reasonable and otherwise in compliance with the rules applicable to tax-exempt organizations. Any private benefit cannot be more than incidental. The arrangement should be approved by the hospital or other tax-exempt organization's governing board, excluding any board members with a personal interest in the arrangement. In addition, certain management contracts will be subject to additional regulatory hurdles if they are located in space financed by tax-exempt bonds.[36]

A Note on State Law Considerations

Each state regulates healthcare and healthcare providers to some degree. Examples of regulations include state medical licensure laws, restrictions on fee splitting, and corporate practice of medicine rules that may limit the ability of certain persons to own or operate business organizations that provide healthcare services. In order to provide comprehensive guidance, lawyers are encouraged to research and consider the laws, rules, and regulations unique to each state in which their healthcare clients conduct business.

Notes

1. 42 U.S.C. § 1395nn(a).
2. *Id.* § 1395nn(h)(5); 42 C.F.R. § 411.351. Certain referrals by pathologists, radiologists, and radiation oncologists are excluded from the definition of referral.
3. 42 U.S.C. § 1395nn(h)(6).
4. 42 C.F.R. § 411.351.
5. 42 U.S.C. § 1395nn(a)(2).
6. 42 C.F.R. § 411.354(b)(5)(i)(A), (b)(5)(iv).
7. *Id.* § 411.354(b)(5)(i)(B).
8. *Id.* § 411.354(b)(2). Note, however, that such interest may be considered as a link in a chain establishing an indirect financial relationship. *Id.*
9. 42 U.S.C. § 1395nn(h).
10. *Id.* § 1395nn(h)(1); 42 C.F.R. § 411.351.
11. 42 C.F.R. § 411.354(c)(i).
12. *Id.* § 411.354(c)(2)(iv)(A), (c)(3)(ii)(C).
13. *Id.* § 411.354(c)(3)(i).
14. *Id.* § 411.354(c)(2)(i).
15. 69 Fed. Reg. 16,054, 16,059 (Mar. 26, 2004).
16. 42 C.F.R. § 411.354(c)(2)(ii).
17. *Id.* § 411.354(c)(2)(iii).
18. If the arrangement is between a hospital and an employed physician, and the hospital participates in an accountable care organization (ACO) that participates in the Medicare Shared Savings Program (MSSP), then the parties should also consider whether the MSSP waivers affect the arrangement. *See* Centers for Medicare and Medicaid Services, Medicare Program; Final Waivers in Connection with the Shared Savings Program (Interim Final Rule), 76 Fed. Reg. 67,992 (Nov. 2, 2011).
19. 42 C.F.R. § 411.357(c). Note that physician recruitment arrangements have a separate safe harbor. *See id.* § 411.357(e).
20. 42 C.F.R. § 411.357(d).
21. *Id.*

22. Arrangements for less than one year may be renewed provided that the terms of the arrangement and the compensation do not change. *Id.* § 411.357(l)(2).

23. *Id.* § 411.357(l).

24. 42 U.S.C. § 1320a-7b(b).

25. Office of Inspector Gen. Advisory Op. No. 09-09 (July 29, 2009).

26. If the arrangement is between a hospital and an employed physician, and the hospital participates in an ACO that participates in the MSSP, then the parties should also consider whether the MSSP waivers affect the arrangement. *See* Centers for Medicare and Medicaid Services, Medicare Program; Final Waivers in Connection with the Shared Savings Program (Interim Final Rule) 76 Fed. Reg. 67,992 (Nov. 2, 2011).

27. 42 C.F.R. § 1001.952(i). This citation is to the regulatory safe harbor. The statute itself also contains an exception for employees. *See* 42 U.S.C. § 1320a-7b(b)(3)(B).

28. 42 C.F.R. § 1001.952(i) (citing 26 U.S.C. § 3121(d)(2)).

29. *Id.* § 1001.952(d).

30. *Id.*

31. *Compliance*, Off. Inspector Gen., https://oig.hhs.gov/compliance (last visited Jan. 28, 2015).

32. 42 U.S.C. § 1320a-7a. Notwithstanding this general prohibition, the OIG has declined to impose sanctions on certain arrangements in which the goals are tied to verifiable cost savings and the arrangement does not incentivize changes in volume or shifts in payer mix that reduce beneficiaries' access to healthcare services. *See, e.g.*, Special Advisory Bulletin, *Gainsharing Arrangements and CMPs for Hospital Payments to Physicians to Reduce or Limit Services to Beneficiaries*, Off. Inspector Gen. (July 1999), http://oig.hhs.gov/fraud/docs/alertsandbulletins/gainsh.htm; Office of Inspector Gen. Advisory Op. No. 12-22 (Dec. 31, 2012), *available at* https://oig.hhs.gov/fraud/docs/advisoryopinions/2012/AdvOpn12-22.pdf; Office of Inspector Gen. Advisory Op. No. 09-06 (June 30, 2009), *available at* http://oig.hhs.gov/fraud/docs/advisoryopinions/2009/AdvOpn09-06.pdf; Office of Inspector Gen. Advisory Op. No. 08-21 (Dec. 8, 2008); Office of Inspector Gen. Advisory Op. No. 01-01 (Jan. 11, 2001), http://oig.hhs.gov/fraud/docs/advisoryopinions/2001/ao01-01.pdf.

33. 42 U.S.C. § 1395u(n).

34. 42 C.F.R. § 414.50(a)(2)(iii).

35. *Id.* § 414.50(a)(i).

36. See, for example, Rev. Proc. 97-13, 1997-5 I.R.B. 18, and related guidance.

Contractual Considerations 2

As described in chapter 1, the Stark Law requires certain arrangements to be set forth in writing and signed by the parties. While the Stark Law does not explicitly require employment agreements to be in writing, and certain arrangements between physicians and healthcare organizations are not subject to the Stark Law, it is generally beneficial to have a written agreement documenting the parties' understanding of, and expectations for, the relationship.[1] While no two arrangements are alike, this chapter provides an overview of key provisions that lawyers should consider when drafting an employment or service agreement between a physician and a healthcare organization. In keeping with the subject matter of this book, this chapter focuses on contractual provisions in the healthcare context[2] and is accompanied by a checklist in chapter 3 of potential terms to include in an agreement. In addition to the provisions described below, some or all of which may be applicable to an agreement depending on the context, readers are encouraged to consider including standard contractual provisions to further memorialize their understanding of an arrangement.[3]

Description of Duties and Services

A contract should describe the services that are expected to be performed. In the physician employment context, the contract often contains a general requirement that the physician engage in the practice of medicine on behalf of his or her employer in the field of the physician's specialty, plus additional provisions covering the physician's hours,[4] call-coverage obligations, and any general administrative duties.[5]

Sample Provision

Establishment of the Employment Relationship (Employment Agreement)
The Company hereby employs the Physician, and the Physician hereby accepts such employment, for the term described herein. The Physician will practice medicine on behalf of the Company in the field of _____. The Company will establish the work schedule for the Physician, including location, hours, and days of employment. The Physician's general on-call requirement will be substantially the same as other full-time physician employees of the Company.

A medical director agreement generally includes a list of duties and expectations specific to the directorship.

Sample Provision

Description of Services

As Medical Director for the [Department/Program], the Physician shall perform the following tasks: (a) oversee and manage the services provided by the [Department/Program] to ensure that such services are provided in accordance with the bylaws and policies and procedures of [Hospital] and [Hospital's] Medical Staff and all applicable professional standards and federal and state laws, rules, and regulations; (b) provide overall medical supervision of allied health professionals assigned to the [Department/Program] and other support personnel assigned to the [Department/Program]; (c) participate in the peer-review process, provide in-service education, attend staff meetings, and perform such other administrative, technical, and support services as may be requested from time to time; (d) participate in [Hospital's] quality-improvement programs for the [Department/Program]; (e) in collaboration with [Hospital], develop clinical and operational protocols and procedures as may be necessary or required for the provision of services to the [Department/Program]; (f) provide such reports as may be reasonably requested by [Hospital]; and (g) take such other actions and perform such other administrative duties as [Hospital] may require from time to time.

Each description of services should strive to satisfy an applicable Stark Law exception or other regulatory requirement that the services be set forth in writing while taking into account circumstances of the position that might require flexibility.[6] In addition, if the parties intend to have an independent-contractor relationship, rather than an employment relationship, the parties should be mindful of IRS rulings and other guidance regarding the indicia of an employment relationship, and the potential liability for misclassifying an employee as an independent contractor.[7]

While in many instances one party is *providing* services and the other party is *receiving* the services, the service provider may have certain expectations of the facility where services will be provided and/or the facilities and equipment available to the provider in the performance of duties and services under the contract, such as an employed physician's expectation that he or she will have a private office.

Sample Provision

Working Facilities

The Company will provide the Physician with such medical and administrative assistance and such other services, equipment, and supplies as are adequate for the performance of the Physician's duties and responsibilities. In addition, the Physician will be provided with a private office during the term of this agreement.

If there are no unusual requests, then a general statement that the entity will provide the necessary personnel, equipment, and supplies for the performance of the provider's duties may be sufficient. If there are any specific expectations of the service provider (such as a certain type of personnel providing assistance), then the parties should consider documenting these obligations to avoid any misunderstandings.

In addition to documenting the services provided by the parties, employment and service agreements should also include a description of the general requirements that may apply, such as maintaining applicable licensure status, maintaining medical staff privileges at one or more hospitals, complying with applicable policies and procedures, and/or being board certified or board eligible in the provider's specialty.

Sample Provision

Duties and Responsibilities

During the term of this agreement, the Physician will at all times (a) be licensed to practice medicine in the State/Commonwealth of _____ without material restrictions or limitations; (b) maintain registration to prescribe controlled substances without any material restrictions or limitations; (c) be a member of the medical staff of each hospital as the Company may direct; (d) be a member of any provider network in which the Company directs the Physician to participate; and (e) participate in Medicare, Medicaid, and other federal and state reimbursement programs, and commercial insurance plans, that the Company may contract with from time to time. The Physician will not be deemed in default of subpart (d) or (e) if the Physician's failure to obtain membership in a provider network is for reasons beyond the Physician's control. The Physician will become board certified in the Physician's specialty no later than _____.

The Physician will perform services under this agreement in accordance with applicable federal and state laws, rules, and regulations; professional standards and codes of ethics; the Company's policies and procedures; and any medical staff bylaws, rules, and regulations of the hospital(s) where the Physician maintains privileges.

Organizations contracting with providers should also consider the circumstances under which a provider should be obligated to notify the organization of any material changes, such as a restriction on the provider's license or the commencement of litigation against the provider.

Sample Provision

Disclosure Obligations

The Physician represents and warrants that he or she has disclosed to the Company all of the following matters to the extent they have occurred and that he or she will disclose to the Company any of the following matters that may occur in the future: (a) any malpractice suit, claim, or settlement and (b) any disciplinary, peer-review, or similar action instituted against the Physician by a healthcare facility, licensure board, governmental agency, or professional society.

The contract can also provide that the failure to meet these requirements is grounds for termination.

Compensation

Compensation is an essential term of any contract. Every agreement should clearly describe how the employee or service provider will be compensated. In the employment context, there are a variety of compensation models, including annual salaries, productivity-based formulas, and base salary/bonus compensation models in which the bonus is either discretionary or based on productivity.[8] Productivity-based compensation and/or bonus formulas can be based on billing or collections. Collection-based formulas are more common and often preferred over billing-based formulas for a variety of reasons. Because a certain percentage of any employer's accounts receivable may be uncollectible, a collection-based formula allows the employer to pay the employee based on amounts actually received and exclude any uncollectible funds in the calculation.

Sample Provision

Fixed Base Compensation

The Company shall pay the Physician annual base compensation of $_____. The base compensation shall be payable in installments in accordance with the Company's policies and procedures, as may be amended from time to time.

Sample Provision

Bonus Compensation

In addition to the base compensation, the Physician shall be entitled to bonus compensation based on the Physician's personal productivity. If in any employment year, the net revenue of the Company attributable to services personally performed by the Physician exceeds the sum of (a) the Physician's base compensation plus (b) the amount of the Company's payroll taxes and expenses on behalf of the Physician and (c) the Company's overhead and other expenses reasonably related to services performed by the Physician, then the Physician shall be entitled to a bonus equal to ___ percent of such excess. The amount of bonus compensation, if any, will be determined by the Company within ___ days of the conclusion of the employment year, and such bonus compensation, less applicable payroll taxes, shall be paid within ___ days of the conclusion of the employment year.

Another example of productivity compensation is a formula based on work relative value units (wRVUs).[9] The Centers for Medicare and Medicaid Services (CMS) assigns each Current Procedural Terminology (CPT) billing code a wRVU, with greater wRVUs generally assigned to procedures deemed more complex or time consuming, or requiring more skill. A wRVU-based compensation formula is intended to determine compensation based on the provider's work effort.[10] Examples of wRVU-based compensation include multiplying a provider's wRVUs during the measuring period by a specific dollar amount (often referred to as a "conversion factor") to determine compensation, establishing compensation based on a minimum number of wRVUs required to earn a base salary, or in a group-practice setting determining each provider's percentage of the total wRVUs generated by all providers in the group and multiplying that percentage by the total amount of money available for the providers' compensation in order to allocate the compensation pool.

Sample Provision

Bonus Compensation (wRVUs)
In addition to base compensation, the Physician shall also be entitled to bonus compensation in the event that the Physician generates more than ___ wRVUs during an employment year (the "Bonus Base"). The Company will determine the amount, if any, of bonus compensation within ___ days of the conclusion of the employment year by multiplying $___ by the amount of wRVUs in excess of the Bonus Base.

Regardless of methodology, if compensation is formula based, the formula should be clearly described in the agreement. It is also helpful to include an example that walks the parties through the formula to demonstrate how it will be applied under the agreement.

Compensation arrangements in service agreements are a function of the type of services provided and applicable legal and regulatory requirements. Medical director arrangements are often based on an hourly rate. On-call arrangements often provide a flat fee per call-coverage period that is applied uniformly among the various physicians or physician groups providing call coverage. Clinical services agreements, such as an exclusive radiology agreement between a radiology group and a hospital, may permit the provider to bill patients directly for the provider's services rather than compensating the provider for such services.

Sample Provision

Hourly Rate
As compensation for the medical director services, Nursing Home shall pay the Physician compensation of $____ per hour of services provided up to a maximum of $____ per year for at least ____ hourse per year, as documented in monthly time sheets signed by the Physician and submitted to the Nursing Home.

Sample Provision

Flat Fee per Call-Coverage Period
As compensation for the call-coverage services, the Hospital shall pay the Group the amount of $____ for each coverage period, as documented in monthly time sheets signed by the Physician providing coverage and submitted by the Group to the Hospital.[11]

Sample Provision

No Compensation Paid (Provider Bills Patients)
The Group shall bill patients for services provided pursuant to this agreement in accordance with the Group's customary practice and usual rates, as well as in accordance with all applicable laws, rules, and regulations.

When drafting compensation provisions, parties and their counsel should be mindful of any potential legal and regulatory implications of such provisions. For example, because the Stark Law generally prohibits physicians from being compensated for services that they did not personally perform, a physician's referrals to other providers generally cannot be included in the compensation pool.[12] In addition, some states have fee-splitting or "mini-Stark" laws that further limit how compensation may be determined. Moreover, certain Stark Law exceptions and Anti-kickback Statute safe harbors require compensation to be fair market value. The parties should maintain documentation that the compensation was fair market value at the time that the arrangement was entered into. Such documentation can include survey data from independent third parties (such as Medical Group Management Association) plus evidence of how such surveys were applied to the specific compensation arrangement. In many instances, parties choose to obtain a formal valuation from a third-party consultant who has experience valuing similar healthcare transactions and understands the nuances of a valuation under the Stark Law, the Anti-kickback Statute, and other applicable laws and regulations.

Term and Termination

Each arrangement should clearly specify the duration of the arrangement, which is generally referred to as the "term." Certain Stark Law exceptions and Anti-kickback Statute safe harbors generally require a minimum term of one year.[13] If the services will not begin immediately upon execution of the agreement by the parties, then the parties may wish to establish a commencement date that is separate from the effective date and that is either a specific date in the future or contingent upon the satisfaction of certain conditions, as applicable.[14] In addition to the term, if the parties contemplate their relationship continuing beyond the initial term, the contract should specify whether the arrangement automatically renews for one or more additional terms or whether it may be renewed by written agreement of the parties.

Sample Provision

Term; Renewal

This agreement shall be for a term of one (1) year commencing on _____ (the "Effective Date"). Thereafter, this agreement shall automatically renew for successive one-year terms commencing on each anniversary of the Effective Date thereafter unless a party provides the other party with written notice of non-renewal at least ___ days before the end of the then current term, or unless this agreement is earlier terminated in accordance with its terms.

In addition to describing the term and any applicable renewal provisions, a contract should describe how the arrangement may be terminated.[15] These provisions generally include one or more of the following types of termination: termination without cause, termination for cause, and immediate termination. In a termination without cause provision, either or both parties to an agreement are permitted to terminate the contract effective after a specified notice period. Because the terminating party is not required to give a reason for terminating the contract, this provision is viewed as reducing the risk of litigation due to wrongful termination.[16]

Sample Provision

Termination without Cause

This agreement may be terminated by either party at any time without cause upon not less than ___ days' prior written notice to the other party.

In a termination for cause provision, either or both parties to an agreement are permitted to terminate the contract due to a breach (or material breach, depending on how the provision is drafted) by the other party. Such clauses often include a time period in which the allegedly breaching party may remedy or "cure" the breach, with termination becoming effective at the expiration of the notice period if the breach is not cured within such time frame. When drafting termination for cause provisions, counsel should consider whether the provision (1) applies to any breach (which could include non-compliance that does not affect the parties in a substantial way), (2) applies to a "material breach" only, or (3) is limited in its application to a breach of certain specified provisions of the contract. Counsel should also address the length of the "cure period" (if any) and how the cure will be determined (e.g., "to the reasonable satisfaction of the non-breaching party").

Sample Provision

Termination for Cause
Either party may terminate this agreement for cause upon ___ days' prior written notice to the other party describing the breach, provided that the party receiving such notice fails to cure such breach to the reasonable satisfaction of the non-breaching party within such time period.

In an immediate termination provision, either or both parties are permitted to terminate immediately based on the occurrence of one or more events, or a change in status of the parties, that substantially interfere with the parties' ability to perform, or desire to receive services under, the agreement. Examples of grounds for immediate termination include a party's failure to meet any terms and conditions that served as prerequisites for the arrangement,[17] a provider's loss of licensure or medical staff privileges, the loss of professional liability coverage, or the bankruptcy or insolvency of a party.

Sample Provision

Immediate Termination
The Group may immediately terminate this agreement in the event the Physician fails to comply with the Group's policies and procedures, is suspended from the Medicare and/or Medicaid programs because of the Physician's improper or illegal conduct, or in the event that the Physician's professional liability insurance is terminated because of acts or omissions by the Physician.

Insurance

The contract should specify what types of insurance[18] each party is required to maintain, the amounts[19] of such coverage, and who will pay for the costs of such coverage. For professional liability insurance, the contract may also specify whether such insurance must be an occurrence policy or a claims-made policy. An occurrence policy covers all incidents that occur during the period that the insurance policy is in effect, regardless of when they are raised. Therefore, even if the policy is not maintained at the time the claim is reported (e.g., if an employed provider has subsequently changed jobs and is now covered by a different employer's insurance), the occurrence policy will provide coverage for the incident (assuming no applicable carve-outs or coverage exceptions exist). A claims-made policy covers the provider for incidents that occur during the period that the insurance policy is in effect and that are reported while the policy is in effect. Incidents occurring prior to the effective date of a claims-made policy are not covered by the policy. If the provider has previously been employed or otherwise provided clinical services, the contract should include a requirement that the provider maintain an extended reporting endorsement (often referred to as "tail coverage") covering the provider's previous acts.[20] The contract should also specify who is responsible for tail coverage for services performed during the term of the agreement upon termination or expiration of the agreement and how long such policy should be maintained.

Sample Provision

Insurance (Employment Agreement)

The Company shall obtain on the Physician's behalf professional liability insurance in amounts deemed reasonable by the Company covering the Company and the Physician for professional services rendered by the Physician pursuant to this agreement. The Company shall maintain such coverage during the term of this agreement. The Company will not cover the period prior to the effective date of this agreement. The Physician is required to obtain coverage for the period prior to such date. Upon termination of this agreement, the Company shall use reasonable efforts to obtain insurance for the Physician for any professional liability claims against the Physician arising from the Physician's performance of services pursuant to this agreement.

Sample Provision

Insurance (Service Agreement)

At the Physician's own expense, the Physician shall maintain professional liability insurance with limits as may be required by the Company. If such coverage is a "claims made" form of insurance and such coverage is terminated, the Physician shall obtain tail insurance covering any event that may have occurred during the term of this agreement. The Physician agrees to notify the Company in writing prior to any cancellation or non-renewal of such insurance. The Physician agrees to provide the Company with a certificate of insurance upon request.

Restrictive Covenants

Among the most common restrictive covenants in healthcare are covenants not to compete, exclusivity provisions, and non-solicitation provisions. In general, covenants not to compete restrict the service provider from providing similar services within the service recipient's market during the term of the agreement between the parties and, in some instances, for a certain period of time after the agreement has been terminated.[21] It is important to be aware of any applicable laws regarding the use of covenants not to compete, as some states prohibit concurrent and/or post-termination restrictive covenants, while others limit them (e.g., by requiring that they be reasonable in time and scope).

Exclusivity provisions require the service provider to provide services exclusively to the service recipient during the term of the agreement. Such provisions are common in hospital contracts for services for an entire department, such as radiology or anesthesia. Non-solicitation provisions prohibit one or both parties from soliciting the other party's employees and/or customers (patients) for a certain period of time.

Sample Provision

Non-solicitation
Each party agrees that during the term of this agreement and for a period of ____ months/____years following termination of this agreement, neither party shall employ, contract with, or offer employment or a contractual relationship to any individual employed by the other party hereto within the ____ period prior to termination of this agreement.

Confidentiality

Confidentiality provisions require one or both parties to keep confidential the other party's proprietary or otherwise sensitive information. This can include patient lists, business plans, intellectual property, and other information that a party does not want disclosed. If one of the parties is a covered entity, as defined by the Health Insurance Portability and Accountability Act of 1996 (HIPAA), and HIPAA-protected information of that party will be used or disclosed in the course of performing under the agreement, then the parties may also need to include a HIPAA business associate agreement.[22] Parties should also consider whether the service provider will have access to information protected by state privacy and security laws and regulations (such as data breach laws) and whether additional contract provisions are required to address such laws.

Sample Provision

Confidentiality

All documents and records related to services rendered under this agreement, or to the operations of the Company, are and shall remain the Company's property. The Physician recognizes and acknowledges that such documents and records are proprietary to the Company, and the Physician will not disclose confidential information without the written consent of the Company except as necessary to perform the Physician's obligations under this agreement and as required by law.

Medical Records

If medical records of a party will be accessed or used by the other party in the course of the arrangement, then in addition to a provision on maintaining the confidentiality of such records as described above, the agreement should specify who owns the medical records and, if applicable, any obligation on the part of the service provider to complete medical records timely and accurately. The service provider may also wish to include language requiring the service recipient to grant the service provider access to such medical records in certain instances, such as in order to defend a claim or in the event of a government investigation.

Sample Provision

Medical Records
The Physician shall complete all medical records timely and accurately. All medical records are the property of the Company. The Company agrees to provide the Physician with copies of appropriate documents requested by the Physician in connection with the Physician's defense of a claim or suit arising from the Physician's provision of services while the Physician was employed by the Company. The Physician shall pay all reasonable expenses incurred by the Company in duplicating such documents.

Dispute Resolution

In the absence of a dispute resolution provision, each party has the right to litigate any dispute that may arise under the agreement. In the alternative, the parties may wish to include a dispute resolution provision in the agreement that requires the parties to submit the dispute to mediation and/or arbitration. While the arguments in favor of and against dispute resolution provisions in healthcare agreements are similar to those in non-healthcare agreements, in the event a dispute resolution provision is included in the agreement, the parties may also wish to identify in the agreement a specific dispute resolution organization with experience in healthcare that will mediate or arbitrate the dispute.

Sample Provision

Dispute Resolution

Any claim arising out of this agreement shall be settled by arbitration in accordance with [insert applicable arbitration association/rules]. Arbitration will be held before ___ arbitrator(s) at a hearing in [location], and judgment upon any award rendered by the arbitrator may be entered in any court having jurisdiction thereof. The parties shall equally pay for the costs of arbitration.

Assignment

Many contracts (whether healthcare related or otherwise) provide that the agreement cannot be assigned by either party without the other party's consent. Such provisions may be advantageous to a party receiving services, particularly if those services are provided by an individual (such as a medical director agreement with an individual physician), as it helps to ensure that the services will be provided only by the party to the original contract. However, many healthcare organizations, particularly hospitals and health systems, are comprised of several related or affiliated entities. For such entities and their counsel, it may be helpful to include an assignment provision that permits the agreement to be assigned to an affiliated entity.

Sample Provision

Assignment (Permitting Unilateral Assignment to an Affiliate)

This agreement may not be assigned by either party without the prior written consent of the other party, provided, however, that the Hospital may assign this agreement to an entity owned by, or under common control with, the Hospital.

Additional Considerations for Service Agreements

If services will be provided to a hospital, skilled-nursing facility, home health agency, hospice, or comprehensive outpatient rehabilitation facility, or a related organization of any of these organizations, and Medicare reimburses the organization for a portion of the cost of the service provider, then the agreement should also give the secretary of the HHS and the Comptroller General the ability to receive, upon request, access to the books and records between the organization and the service provider.[23]

Additional Considerations for Employment Agreements

In addition to the provisions described above, most of which apply to both service agreements and employment agreements, employment relationships often entail a consideration of additional factors, such as federal and state employment laws and other concerns. Below is a general overview of some employment-related provisions for consideration when drafting employment agreements with physicians. In addition, chapter 4 includes sample terms for a term-sheet between a physician and a potential employer.

Employee Benefits
The agreement should describe any benefits that the employee is entitled to, such as paid time off, insurance (e.g., health, dental, disability, and/or life insurance),[24] continuing medical education, licensing and membership fees and dues, medical journals, and cell phone expenses.

Consideration for Admission as an Owner
For employment agreements with physician practices and physicians, the parties may wish to specify whether the employee will be considered for admission as an owner at some point in the future. From the

employee's perspective, such provisions provide the physician with a path to ownership and relative certainty that the issue will be discussed by a certain date, usually two to three years (but sometimes as little as one year) after the physician begins providing services for the practice. From the employer's perspective, the agreement should be clear that ownership will be *considered* but is not *guaranteed*. It can also be helpful to include any special post-ownership compensation provisions, the purchase price for any buy-in or the formula for calculating the purchase price, the expected percentage ownership that the physician will receive, and whether such ownership will entitle the physician to voting and/or management rights.[25]

Assignment of Meaningful Use Incentive Payments

Under the Medicare and Medicaid Electronic Health Record (EHR) Incentive Programs,[26] eligible professionals and hospitals receive payments by demonstrating their meaningful use of EHR technology. Providers are required to attest to meaningful use each year in order to receive an incentive and to avoid a payment adjustment. Providers may assign the right to receive payment; however, such assignment is not mandatory. Employers providing the EHR that will serve as the basis for the incentive payment should consider including an assignment of the right to receive incentive payments to the employer.

Summary

Employment and service agreements between physicians and healthcare organizations require the parties and their counsel to navigate a variety of federal and state laws, rules, and regulations in addition to addressing standard contractual terms. This book is designed to provide the reader with a general overview of common legal and regulatory issues involved in physician employment contracts and service agreements with healthcare organizations for clinical and medico-administrative services. Readers are encouraged to conduct their own independent research and avail themselves of seminars, conferences, journals, and other educational materials to gain additional insight and understanding into this complex and evolving area of law.

Notes

1. Because ACOs participating in the MSSP must submit documents evidencing providers' obligations to the ACO, hospitals participating in an ACO under the MSSP who employ physicians should consider having a written agreement with employed physicians to document ACO obligations, such as term, ACO-related duties and services (and compensation for same), distribution of the ACO's shared savings and losses, and applicable language regarding the MSSP waivers.

2. Entities participating in ACOs should also consider whether additional language is required (such as language applicable to ACOs participating in the MSSP), either in the employment agreement or in a separate joinder agreement between the organization and the provider. *See, e.g.*, note 1.

3. Examples of standard contractual terms, often referred to as "boilerplate," include waiver of breach, severability, modification, further assurances, governing law, notice, integration, construction, counterparts, and survival clauses.

4. Many contracts will simply require the physician to provide services "on a full-time basis." Physicians with specific restrictions on their schedule or those providing services on a part-time basis should consider including a description of the days/times during which they are available.

5. Employment agreements for professional medical services should also state whether the relationship is exclusive or whether the provider is permitted to provide outside services. For example, some arrangements require the employee to provide all professional medical services through the employer but permit the employee to provide nonmedical services, such as serving as an independent medical consultant, outside of the scope of such employment.

6. For example, an entity with multiple offices might state that the physician will provide services to the entity at such locations as may be required based on the needs of the entity, rather than assigning the physician to a particular office.

7. *See, e.g., Independent Contractor (Self-Employed) or Employee?*, Internal Rev. Serv., http://www.irs.gov/Businesses/Small-Businesses-&-Self-Employed/Independent-Contractor-Self-Employed-or-Employee (last updated Oct. 2, 2014).

8. In physician group practices, compensation for physician-owners may also be based on each physician's net revenue (i.e., net collections) less his or her direct expenses and less an allocation of the practice's overhead. While this method can also be used for employed physicians, physicians without an established patient base may find it difficult to achieve sufficient net revenue to make the model worthwhile. Among the details to consider when drafting and negotiating collection-based compensation models are how direct expenses will be defined and how general overhead costs will be allocated among the group's physicians. An example of a potential issue is whether all physicians will be responsible for the salary and expenses of a physician assistant that is used by only some members of the group.

9. This book contains only a brief overview of wRVUs. Note that relative value units are also assigned based on practice expense and malpractice overhead. In addition, the Centers for Medicare and Medicaid Services publishes a Geographic Practice Cost Index to adjust relative value units for various geographic regions.

10. As compared to revenue-based compensation models that are designed to compensate the provider based on billings or collections.

11. See Advisory Opinion 12-15 (Oct. 30, 2012) for a discussion of the Anti-kickback Statute implications of per diem payments for call-coverage arrangements.

12. *See, e.g.*, 42 C.F.R. § 411.352(i) (bonus compensation in group practices).

13. Parties negotiating management contracts in property financed by tax-exempt bonds (such as an exclusive agreement to provide all ob-gyn services in a nonprofit hospital) may wish to limit the term in order to comply with applicable IRS guidance on such arrangements. *See, e.g.*, Rev. Proc. 97-13, 1997-5 I.R.B. 18.

14. For example, if the arrangement requires the provider to be a member of a specific hospital's medical staff, then the commencement date could be established with reference to that condition.

15. While the "term" section of a contract memorializes the parties' agreement concerning the duration of the contract, most contracts nonetheless include termination provisions.

16. While parties may view termination without cause provisions as reducing the risk of litigation, the terminated party may nonetheless bring a claim for wrongful termination or take other legal action.

17. See *supra* Description of Duties and Services in this chapter.

18. In addition to professional liability (malpractice) insurance, some contracts require the parties to maintain general commercial liability insurance or other types of insurance, based on the types of services provided and the context in which they are provided.

19. Note that some states have mandatory minimums for insurance.

20. In some instances, an employed provider's new employer will obtain a policy covering the new employee's prior acts. This is referred to as "nose coverage."

21. Note that most covenants not to compete are accompanied by a provision permitting the party seeking to enforce the covenant to obtain injunctive relief.

22. In general, employees are considered members of a covered entity's workforce, in which event the covered entity is not required to have a business associate agreement with the employee.

23. 42 U.S.C. § 1395x(v)(1)(I). For an example of how this provision is worded, see 42 U.S.C. § 1395x(v)(1)(I)(i)–(ii).

24. This is in addition to professional liability (malpractice) insurance described *supra* in this chapter.

25. It may be more advantageous to reduce post-ownership compensation rather than have a dollar buy-in that the new owner may be required to pay with after-tax dollars. Parties are encouraged to work with both legal counsel and their tax advisors to determine the proper structure.

26. 42 C.F.R. pt. 495. The EHR Incentive Programs were implemented pursuant to the Health Information Technology for Economic and Clinical Health Act, often referred to as the "HITECH Act," part of the American Recovery and Reinvestment Act of 2009.

Contract Checklist 3

Below is a checklist of potential provisions to be included in an employment or service agreement based on the provisions discussed in this book. Readers are encouraged to adapt the list to their needs and to include additional provisions as may be warranted by the arrangement.[1]

❏ Party names and addresses (use correct legal names)
❏ Effective date
❏ Commencement date for services, if different from effective date
❏ Description of duties and services (include any conditions to the commencement/continuation of services, such as maintaining licensure, medical staff membership, etc.)
❏ Compensation
❏ Term and termination (include renewal provision, if applicable)
❏ Insurance
❏ Restrictive covenants (covenant not to compete; non-solicitation; exclusivity)
❏ Confidentiality
   ❏ HIPAA business associate agreement (if required)

❏   State privacy and/or security (e.g., data protection/breach) provisions (if applicable)
❏   Medical records
❏   Dispute resolution
❏   Assignment
❏   Access to books and records
❏   Employee benefits
❏   Consideration for admission as an owner
❏   Assignment of meaningful use incentive payments
❏   ACO provisions

Note

1. *See* Chapter 2, note 3.

Sample Term-
Sheet Provisions

4

Below is a checklist of potential provisions to be included in a term-sheet for an employment agreement based on the provisions discussed in this book. Readers are encouraged to adapt the list to their needs and to include additional provisions as may be warranted by the arrangement.

- ❏ Employment status (e.g., full- or part-time basis)
- ❏ Compensation (including any additional payments such as a signing bonus or relocation expenses)
- ❏ Title for administrative services (e.g., Medical Director of _____)
- ❏ Term
- ❏ Insurance
- ❏ Restrictive covenants (covenant not to compete; non-solicitation; exclusivity)
- ❏ Employee benefits
  - ❏ Vacation
  - ❏ Sick time
  - ❏ Holidays
  - ❏ Expense reimbursement
  - ❏ Pension plan

❏   Insurance

❏   Consideration for admission as an owner

About the Author

Pamela H. Del Negro is a member of Robinson+Cole's Health Law Group, where she advises institutional providers, including hospitals and ambulatory surgery centers, as well as physician practice groups, community providers, and other health care entities on health care issues and general corporate matters. She provides legal counsel on a full range of transactional and regulatory health law issues, including co-management arrangements; compliance plans; the acquisition and merger of medical entities; Medicare and Medicaid fraud and abuse and the Stark law; hospital affiliations; the privacy and security of personal health information; corporate governance; private placements; and contracting. She also works with clients on managed care contracting, the corporate practice of medicine issues, clinical integration and antitrust issues, and the structuring and acquisition of electronic health records technology, including the negotiation and documentation of software agreements.

Prior to joining Robinson+Cole, Ms. Del Negro was affiliated with Bershtein, Volpe & McKeon P.C., where she practiced health care and corporate law. She was managing editor of the *Connecticut Insurance Law Journal* and president of the Health Law Interest Group while earning her J.D. at the University of Connecticut School of Law.